WHEN I GROW UP

DINOSAURS

FIRST EDITION

Published in 2021 by
GREEN CAT BOOKS
19 St Christopher's Way
Pride Park
Derby
DE24 8JY

www.green-cat.shop

Copyright © 2021 Jacqueline Theodosi
ISBN: 978-1-913794-32-3

HI, MY NAME IS REX AND I AM A DINOSAUR!
DO YOU KNOW WHAT TYPE OF DINOSAUR I AM?
I AM A TYRANNOSAURUS REX!

RAAWWRR!

WHEN I GROW UP, I WILL WEIGH AS **MUCH** AS 7000 KILOGRAMS.

THAT IS EVEN **HEAVIER** THAN AN ELEPHANT!

I WILL BE VERY BIG! I CAN GROW UP TO BE
12 METRES LONG.

THAT IS AS **LONG** AS A BUS!

I WILL HAVE A POWERFUL JAW WITH LOTS OF RAZOR-SHARP TEETH!
MY JAW WILL BE SO POWERFUL THAT I COULD **CRUSH** A CAR!

CHOMP,
CHOMP,
CHOMP!

MY ARMS WILL ONLY BE SMALL, BUT I CAN STILL USE
THEM IF OTHER DINOSAURS GET TOO CLOSE.

HI, MY NAME IS RAPTOR!
DO YOU KNOW WHAT TYPE OF DINOSAUR I AM?
I AM A VELOCIRAPTOR!

SCREEEEECH. SCREECH!

WHEN I GROW UP, I WILL HAVE **THREE SHARP**, CURLED CLAWS AND A TALON ON MY BACK LEGS.

I WILL HAVE FEATHERS, JUST LIKE A BIRD BUT I WILL NOT BE ABLE TO FLY LIKE ONE.

FULLY GROWN, I WILL WEIGH
45 KILOGRAMS,
THAT IS AROUND THE SAME
AS A **WOLF!**

I WILL HAVE LONG, MUSCULAR BACK LEGS
TO HELP ME RUN **FAST**!

ZROOOMM!

HI, MY NAME IS CERA! DO YOU KNOW WHAT TYPE OF DINOSAUR I AM?
I AM A TRICERATOPS!

SNOOOORT SNOOORT!

WHEN I GROW UP, I WILL HAVE A MOUTH LIKE A BEAK AND HAVE AROUND **800 TEETH!**

THESE LITTLE TEETH WILL HELP ME **CHOMP** ON PLANTS AND LEAVES.

MMMM. YUMMY!

AS AN ADULT TRICERATOPS,

I WILL BE AS **BIG** AS,

AN
ELEPHANT!

I WILL HAVE A **SHARP** HORN ON MY NOSE AND TWO ON THE TOP OF MY HEAD, WHICH I CAN USE TO DEFEND MYSELF.

I WILL ALSO HAVE A **BIG** BONEY FRILL ON MY NECK WHICH WILL ACT LIKE A SHIELD.

HOW COOL IS THAT?!

DID YOU KNOW THAT THE WORD "TRICERATOPS" MEANS "THREE-HORNED FACE", JUST LIKE MINE!

HI! MY NAME IS DIPLO! DO YOU KNOW WHAT TYPE OF DINOSAUR I AM? I AM A DIPLODOCUS!

GROOOWWL!

WHEN I GROW UP, I WILL BE ONE OF THE **LONGEST** DINOSAURS, REACHING UP TO **33 METRES** LONG!

MY **REALLY LONG** NECK
REACH THE LEAVES
I WILL ALSO HAVE
WHICH I
BALANCE BECAUSE

WILL HELP ME TO
ON TALL TREES.
A **REALLY LONG** TAIL,
NEED FOR
OF MY LONG NECK.

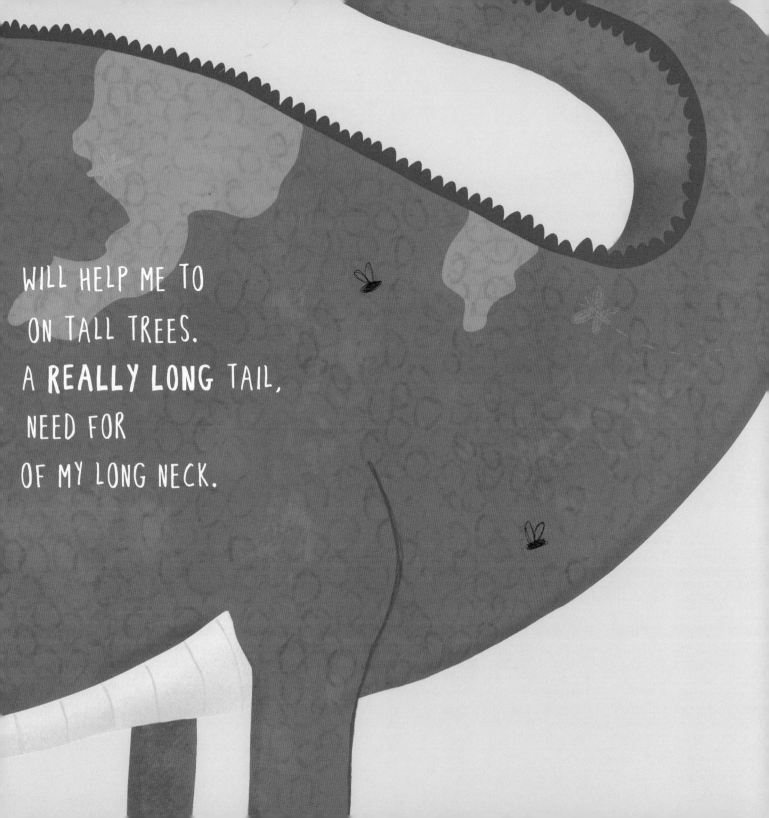

I WILL HAVE **FIVE** SETS OF TEETH!

EACH TOOTH CAN BE REPLACED
WITHIN 35 **DAYS.**

HI! MY NAME IS STEGO! DO YOU KNOW WHAT TYPE OF DINOSAUR I AM?
I AM A STEGOSAURUS!

GRUNT, GRUNT, GRUNT!

WHEN I GROW UP, I WILL HAVE A **STRONG.**
SPIKED TAIL WHICH I WILL USE TO DEFEND MYSELF
FROM OTHER DINOSAURS.

MY HEAD WILL STAY QUITE SMALL AND
MY BRAIN WILL BE THE SIZE OF A **PLUM!**

EVEN FULLY GROWN, I WILL MOVE **VERY** SLOWLY.

I WILL WALK ON ALL FOURS, BUT MY FRONT LEGS WILL BE **SHORTER** THAN MY BACK LEGS.

I WILL BE AS **LONG** AS 6.4 METRES.

WHICH IS AS **LONG** AS A PYTHON SNAKE!

HIIISSSSS!

WHEN I GROW UP, I WILL HAVE A LONG BEAK WITH **90 TEETH!** MY TEETH WILL HELP ME CATCH FISH TO EAT.

EACH OF MY WINGS WILL BE ONE METRE **WIDE**.
THAT IS AS **LONG** AS A BASEBALL BAT!

I WILL BE VERY **BIRD-LIKE**,
BUT I WILL NOT GROW FEATHERS LIKE A BIRD.

MY WINGS ARE MADE OF SKIN,
JUST LIKE BAT WINGS.

BUT GUESS WHAT?...
I AM NOT REALLY A DINOSAUR!

NOW IT IS **YOUR** TURN! WHAT ARE YOU GOING TO BE LIKE WHEN YOU GROW UP?

About the author

Jacqueline lives in Burton on Trent, Staffordshire with her husband Andreas and her two children, Stavros and Christalla. She works as a clinical photographer in the NHS, but had always dreamt of writing her own book.

Inspiration came from her young son's obsession with dinosaurs and the joy that reading to her children brought.

For details of our other books, or to submit your own manuscript please visit
www.green-cat.shop

Green Cat Books

Printed in Great Britain
by Amazon